What Others Are Saying
LINKED® for Educators

"As a campus minister, I work with many different personality types on a daily basis from students to parents to faculty and staff. Having *LINKED® for Educators Quick Guide to Personalities* as a ready guide and refresher on the personalities is extremely useful and its easy-to-understand layout makes digesting the handy tips for dealing with the personalities a quick and stress-free exercise. I highly recommend this short guide for anyone practicing in the people-oriented professions."

~Dr. Henry W. Clary
Dean of Spiritual Formation
Bluefield College

"Understanding how to accept and celebrate different personalities in the classroom can be a game changer for both teachers and students. Linda Gilden and Linda Goldfarb offer a superb succinct guide to recognizing and responding to the mobilizer, socializer, stabilizer, and organizer in each educational setting. Imagine the empowerment this knowledge can bring as teachers capitalize on the strengths of each student!"

~Dalene Parker, Ed.D., NBCT
Educator and Author

"Like an excellent teacher's aide, this practical handbook by personality consultants, Linda Gilden and Linda Goldfarb, easily makes a teacher's job more efficient and effective. Learning increases exponentially when instructors teach to their students' strengths and this book shows you how."

~PeggySue Wells, bestselling author of 28 titles
including *Rediscovering Your Happily Ever After* and
Bonding With Your Child Through Boundaries

"Just think how exciting it would be if you could find out what type of personalities are sitting in your classroom as soon as possible! Wouldn't that make your job of teaching easier? Would it make a difference in how you presented your lessons? Thanks to the two Lindas, the *LINKED for Educators Quick Guide to Personalities,* can make that happen. I spent 27 years in the high school classroom and coaching football, baseball, and golf, so I know how important it is to understand the personalities in the classroom and on the playing field. Don't miss this chance to make a lifetime IMPACT on your students and players, by utilizing the strategies and ideas presented in the LINKED for Educators Quick Guide to Personalities."

~Michael D. Miller, Retired Educator/ Coach-27 years San Antonio.

"In *LINKED for Educators Quick Guide to Personalities,* Linda Gilden and Linda Goldfarb take the guesswork out of understanding and working with students and other teachers. They offer a treasure of tools for the readers. Teachers who read this book and use the tools can have a more successful school year with happier, more productive students. I highly recommend that principals or parent-teacher associations provide a copy of this book for every teacher and that churches do the same for their Sunday school, Bible study, and Vacation Bible School teachers."

~Yvonne Ortega, LPC (Licensed Professional Counselor), Speaker, Author, Former secondary and college teacher, Sunday school, Bible study, and VBS teacher

"The knowledge of the personalities is invaluable to every educator. Over the many years that I have applied this information, I have found that it has helped me to better understand and relate to my students, plan lessons that appeal to all students, and discipline my students with a heart for who they were. If you want to revolutionize your teaching practices, read this book and put this information into play!"

~Andrea Chevalier
Elementary Principal at Logos Preparatory
Academy, Sugar Land, Texas

"To know a child is to better teach that child. A child's personality in many ways determines how he learns best. As a teacher with 41 years experience I have learned that my students learn differently. Learning more about their personality gives a teacher direction to help diversify her teaching to meet the needs of that individual child."

~Sheila Sistare
Middle School Educator

"As a lifelong educator, there's nothing more important than relationships. As Margaret Wheatley once said, "People are the solution to the problems that confront us." Thank you Linda Gilden and Linda Goldfarb for your thoughtful insights about the power of personality. When we better understand ourselves we're far more effective in the ways we relate to others. This book should be on every teacher's desk!"

~Dr. Russell Booker
Superintendent of Spartanburg (SC)
County School District Seven

LINKED
for
EDUCATORS

QUICK GUIDE
TO
PERSONALITIES

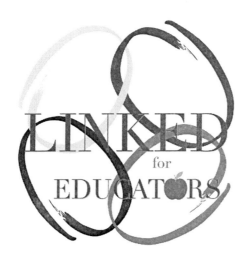

LINKED

for

EDUCATORS

QUICK GUIDE TO PERSONALITIES

Maximizing Classroom Connections
One Link at a Time

Linda Gilden and Linda Goldfarb

Bold Vision Books
PO Box 2011
Friendswood, Texas 77549

Copyright © Linda Gilden and Linda Goldfarb 2018

ISBN 9781946708304
Library of Congress Control Number:2018963080

LINKED® is a registered trademark symbol

Published by Bold Vision Books, PO Box 2011,
Friendswood, Texas 77549
www.boldvisionbooks.com

Logo and Cover Design by Linda Goldfarb
Emojis Design by Jonathan Bishop

Published in the United States of America.

Dedication

Dedicated to all educators and those who
sit under their teaching. May the knowledge
of the personalities benefit you and give you
a better understanding of your peers, your
students, and yourself.

Table of Contents

Introduction

Among all the dynamics of a successful classroom, the personalities of teachers and their students could be the greatest. Do you wonder why some students seem so eager to learn and others have a hard time grasping even the simplest concept? Do those differences bother you? Have you considered whether or not the *differences* in your students could change based on *your* perspective? They can.

Educator-to-student connections are often prevented from growing because of the *perceived* motives behind the actions of others. The main reason? Because you do not understand why your students do what they do and they have no clue about you. In a learning situation, the student's comprehension and grasp of the lessons is influenced not only by his or her personality, but also by the personality of the teacher and how he or she relates to him or her.

Research at Griffith University found personality is more important than intelligence when it comes to success in education: "Dr Arthur Poropat from Griffith's School of Applied Psychology has conducted the largest ever reviews of personality and academic performance. He based these reviews on the fundamental personality factors (conscientiousness, openness, agreeableness, emotional stability, and extraversion) and found conscientiousness and openness have the biggest influence on academic success."[1]

The Poropat study affirms that understanding personalities in the classroom can help teachers identify who they are teaching and better educate their students according to their personality strengths and weaknesses. Each of us is different, created with a unique personality that influences our actions and reactions. Discovering and acting on those differences will result in a productive learning environment for both the teacher and the student.

Teachers, whether in a classroom, at home, or in some other setting, are responsible for making sure all students have the best opportunity to learn. When asked the question, "What does a good learning environment look like?" some of the answers include:

> "A well-appointed classroom should have all the basics with enough supplies for every student."

> "We converted our garage to a schoolroom so our children could totally focus on their work."

"My children have always learned best when they knew their teacher cared about them."

"Students need to feel safe and respected in their learning environments."

These answers about what constitutes an optimal learning environment are all true. Most people, however, never think to mention the personality of the teacher or the student. Regardless of the physical situation of the "classroom," without a positive, encouraging atmosphere, prime learning can't take place.

St. Paul says, "If it is possible, as far as it depends on you, live at peace with everyone." The key phrase is in the middle – "as far as it depends on you." We have a responsibility in our relationships— teacher to student, friend to friend, family member to family member, coworker to coworker, etc. – to do everything we can to live peacefully. One of the core elements to living peacefully with others is understanding the personalities.

This *LINKED® for Educators Quick Guide to Personalities* helps you understand your personality, the personalities of other teachers, and the personalities of your students. Knowing how to approach the different personalities in your classroom and the best way to encourage students to study and learn, gives teachers like you, an advantage when you step into the classroom. When you understand your actions and reactions are a result of your natural personality traits combined with your life experiences, and it is the same for your students, your classroom connections will be strengthened one link at a time.

Connecting with others through the personalities opens the door to greater opportunities in every aspect of your life. Not only the classroom, but family, friends, coworkers, and even strangers will benefit from your newly found perception. Here are the four basic personality types we cover in LINKED®.

Mobilizer

Get-it-done

Socializer

Life-of-the-party

Stabilizer

Keep-it-peaceful

Organizer

Everything-in-order

You may be familiar with these personality types by other names. Hippocrates called them choleric, sanguine, phlegmatic, and melancholy based on an interpretation of body fluids. Others have given them animal names such as lion, otter, golden retriever, and beaver. Then you have those who use terms such as upholder, obligor, questioner, and rebel or letters such as DISC. (These letters stand for Dominance, Influence, Steadiness, and Compliance.)

This *LINKED® for Educators Quick Guide to Personalities* uses the words Mobilizer, Socializer, Stabilizer, and

Organizer. In every method of assessment there is a powerful personality, a playful personality, a peaceful personality, and a purposeful personality. No matter what you call them, each of the four corresponds with one of these descriptions.

Who needs a *LINKED for Educators Quick Guide to Personalities*?

- Teachers who value student-teacher relationships and want to make them stronger.
- Teachers who want to understand how to help students learn more easily and quickly.
- Teachers who desire information in a nutshell.
- Teachers who engage with students on a regular basis.
- Teachers who want to connect with parents and employers.
- Teachers who are life coaches and pretty much everyone who educates others.

Why does understanding personalities work?

- People need people, and all people are not alike.
- Every teacher has met students they don't get along with.
- Every teacher has met a student who makes him or her happy.

- Every teacher has met fellow teachers who makes him or her feel uncomfortable.
- Knowing why teachers respond to students differently strengthens classroom connections.

And who stands to benefit?

Everyone. We're created for relationships. No matter who we are, where we live, or what we do for a living, we interact with other people every day. And as St. Paul suggested, we should try to get along with everybody.

Sounds wonderful on paper, right? Yet it takes intentionality. Finding out more about yourself, how you relate to others, and meshing your personalities to create relationships that last—takes work. But, it's worth it. You can do this.

"A good teacher can inspire hope, ignite the imagination, and instill a love of learning."

~Brad Henry

26th Governor of Oklahoma

Identify Your Personality
(who you are)

You may have heard about personalities for many years. Yet perhaps you've never had the opportunity to know what personality you are and how it applies to your relationships. You may have never considered that knowing your personality and the personalities of your students would make you a better teacher. Perhaps you've taken several personality assessments yet they didn't pinpoint how to manage relationships in a nutshell. LINKED will do that for you. It only takes a few minutes to determine what your dominant and secondary personalities are. The best way to figure it out is to take the LINKED® Personality Assessment below.

Circle the answers that describe how you react most often. Go with your first thought, be as honest as you can, and don't over think your answers. For best results, don't consider which is the good or bad, better or best choice. Mark one answer per question. (Phrases or words in parentheses can be substituted when giving assessment to students.)

1. **You've been assigned a project to complete in two weeks. You**

     a.   get it done right away, even if you have to stay up late.

    b. procrastinate but finish well at the last minute.

    c. have a challenge finishing as you want the project perfect.

    d. take your time, finishing at an easy pace.

2. **Friends would describe you as**
    a. bold and to the point.
    b. fun and entertaining.
    c. cautious and detail-oriented.
    d. likable and easy going.

3. **You find yourself in a conversation with neighbors or coworkers. You**
    a. laugh sometimes and enjoy joining in.
    b. listen and contribute only when needed.
    c. might interrupt with a solution for most problems.
    d. listen and offer encouragement.

4. **The most important thing to have in life is**
    a. peace.
    b. perfection.
    c. fun.
    d. control.

5. **When it comes to friends, you**
    a. have never met a stranger.
    b. see little need for friends.
    c. make friends cautiously.
    d. are easy to get along with.

6. **When choosing a place to eat, you**
   a. act spontaneously.
   b. change your mind often.
   c. have particular places in mind.
   d. don't have a preference.

7. **Your ideal weekend would include**
   a. traveling to a new place.
   b. having quality time with your spouse or a friend.
   c. learning a new skill.
   d. having a pajama day.

8. **When you are stressed, you**
   a. take a nap.
   b. call a friend and go shopping.
   c. get away to a secluded spot to recharge.
   d. exercise more.

9. **If you look in your closet you will see**
   a. all the pants together, shirts together, and shoes lined up in order.
   b. bright colors and fun patterns.
   c. multiple outfits with all pieces hanging together.
   d. a lot of comfortable clothes.

10. **When a child is hurting, you**
    a. empathize with him or her.
    b. listen intently to him or her.
    c. tell him or her to be strong and get back into life.

    d. try to make him or her feel better by suggesting something fun.

11. When you are in a crowd, you
    a. enjoy all your new best friends.
    b. wish you could hurry up and get home and put your feet up.
    c. retreat to the perimeter to talk to someone you already know.
    d. work the crowd to identify contacts.

12. People often say you are
    a. controlling.
    b. fun-loving.
    c. self-disciplined.
    d. laid back.

13. Driving to work, you see a man knock a lady over and then flee. You would most likely
    a. call the police and jump to the lady's aid.
    b. park the car, call police, and wait.
    c. pass on by hoping she's okay.
    d. ask if she is all right and text friends to tell what you saw.

14. Getting on an elevator to go four floors, you
    a. waste no time in starting a conversation with those already on.
    b. move to the back corner and hope the elevator is fast.

c. smile and stand quietly.

d. push the button for your floor and ask the others which floor they're on.

15. **When unexpected company knocks at your door, you**
    a. turn around and shout "Party!"
    b. invite them in and immediately begin tidying up.
    c. tell them it's good to see them, but you have a headache, hoping they won't stay long.
    d. invite them in, control the short visit, then stand and bid them good-bye.

16. **While lying in the hammock by the lake, you**
    a. take a nap easily.
    b. make a check-list for errands.
    c. invite a friend to join you.
    d. analyze the clouds wondering if rain is coming.

17. **Your parents are coming for a visit. You**
    a. rush around making sure everything is in place and clean.
    b. brief the family on how to act and what to do.
    c. decide the house is clean enough.
    d. call all the relatives letting them know about the visit.

18. When given the choice you prefer
a. to lead.
b. to serve.
c. to research.
d. to entertain.

19. When you are sad, you
a. read a book.
b. tell a friend.
c. work on a project.
d. take a nap.

20. When given the opportunity to voice your opinion
a. you speak right up.
b. give your opinion and more.
c. choose your words carefully.
d. you say very few words.

21. If you were a piece of a puzzle, you would be
a. the corners.
b. the bright flowers.
c. the straight edges.
d. the background.

22. In life, you tend to be
a. playful.
b. purposeful.
c. powerful.
d. peaceful.

23. Your car of choice would be
    a.   economical and safe.
    b.   comfortable and easy to maintain.
    c.   sporty and fun.
    d.   stylish and dependable.

24. You prefer life
    a.   done the right way.
    b.   done the fast way.
    c.   done the easy way.
    d.   done the fun way.

25. How would your family describe you?
    a.   competitive.
    b.   cautious.
    c.   committed.
    d.   carefree.

26. Your co-workers describe you as
    a.   results-oriented.
    b.   service-oriented.
    c.   detail-oriented.
    d.   pleasure-oriented.

"Good teachers know how to bring
out the best in students."
                    ~Charles Kuralt

Linking Your Chain

Linking your chain is your first step in discovering more about who you are. Circle your answers on the Assessment Key in the back of the book and record the numbers there. Transfer your totals below on the line designated by the name.

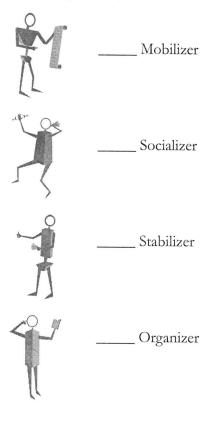

_____ Mobilizer

_____ Socializer

_____ Stabilizer

_____ Organizer

The highest number is your dominant personality. The next highest number is your secondary personality. Write them below.

Dominant _____

Secondary _____

Please note: You may find yourself in several categories and wonder if you are really just too mixed up to be anything. The answer is a resounding NO! You were designed differently for a reason. Some of us are no-assessment-needed, hands-down one distinct personality, while others may exhibit characteristics of more than one. But for the most part, you will have a dominant personality. And so will your students.

Identifying the Personalities of Your Students

If you are new to the study of the personalities, you may think it difficult to determine the personalities of your students. But with a little help here, you should be able to place them into the correct personality group without any trouble. Please note, LINKED is not a labeling system. It's an avenue of understanding that will take your teaching to the next level. And, in the process, everyone in your classroom will benefit as well.

You could use the questionnaire above and have your students take the questionnaire as a group. You read the questions and they respond on a sheet of paper. Reassure the students their answers will not be made known to the class; it's for self-discovery and for you to understand them better as individuals. It's important to give students time to tally their scores. Let them know before you start they will have ten to fifteen minutes to complete and tally their scores. When they are finished, enlighten them as to what you have learned from this quick guide about the characteristics of their personality types. Once complete, take up the papers so you have the benefit of knowing how they scored. Reassure the students it's their choice to share their personality findings with the class.

Another option would be to start each class with a personality-focused question of the day, as a bellringer. If you choose this option, it's important to gather the info without compromising the identity of the student. Some students wait to see how someone else answers then agree, thinking one answer is better than another. To ensure authentic answers, hand out an index card asking the students to write their names on them and to write down the answer to "today's question" (already written on the board) and turn it in to you. Some questions you may consider are:

- Would you describe yourself as the get-it-done person, the life-of-the-party person, the keep-it-peaceful person, or the everything-in-order-person?
- When you get home from school, when do you do your homework? Right away, before going to bed, the next morning at school, or when you're reminded to?
- Did you enjoy your homework assignment last night to write a paper on your family genealogy? Why or why not? (Answers will give you a clue to the study habits of students and if they enjoy research, prefer to do the research themselves, find other people to give information, or just really didn't have a lot of interest in the assignment.)
- Do you make new friends easily, cautiously, reservedly, or rarely?
- Do you like spontaneity and fun?

- Are you a good storyteller, or do you think stories are just for those who don't have anything else to do but make up fairytales?
- When you are in a group, do you do all the talking, talk only when people pay attention, think carefully before you talk, or prefer listening to others?

You could also adapt questions from the teacher questionnaire in the section above this one. Since this method uses one question at different times, keep track of their index cards in a box or folder. It won't take long to figure out which students are Mobilizers, Socializers, Stabilizers, or Organizers.

We have included a Get-to-know-you Quick Student Questionnaire at the back of this book and on our website as a free download. You can use it at the beginning of the year for everyone or when you have new students join mid-term. Please check it out under the resource tab at www.LinkedPersonalities. com.

Teacher's Key for the Get-to-know-you Quick Student Questionnaire

Mobilizer: 1a, 2a, 3a, 4d, 5b, 6a, 7b
Socializer: 1b, 2c, 3c, 4a, 5d, 6c, 7a
Stabilizer: 1c, 2d, 3d, 4b, 5a, 6d, 7d
Organizer: 1d, 2b, 3b, 4c, 5c, 6b, 7c

Now, let's take a look at each personality and connect the links.

You might be a MOBILIZER if...

- You love to live life the fast way.

- You're a gifted teacher who loves challenges.

- You tend to be focused, direct, and to the point.

- You demand loyalty and appreciation.

- You're distracted/disturbed when the classroom is out of control.

- You like having your hands in several projects.

- Exercise and hard work relax you.

- You want all your students to succeed.

Mobilizers are the movers and shakers of the world. They set their goals and then move full speed ahead to accomplish them. Mobilizers make great teachers, but, they can come across as pushy and having too high of expectations for the Stabilizer and Socializer students. Be sure to give plenty of time for assignments to be completed. In other occupations, you see Mobilizers as committee chairmen or heads of companies. In education, they lead their classrooms powerfully in a way that other teachers and parents appreciate. If you want something done, the Mobilizer is a good choice for making that happen.

Before the school year begins, the Mobilizer teacher has goals and lesson plans in place. She has studied the class roll to see if she recognizes any of the students. She has talked to former teachers to see how she can best serve the incoming class. The Mobilizer makes a checklist so she knows what each school day will look like. Yes, all teachers look at their rosters, but I don't know if they think about the personality of each student? Probably not! The good thing is, you're changing that.

"Learning I was a Mobilizer changed my life," says Darcy, fifth-grade elementary school teacher. "People called me bossy, but I didn't understand why. Students called me mean, but I never saw myself that way. I just want students to learn every part of every lesson. I didn't understand that out of all my students only a few embraced my personal learning style and most needed a little extra direction. Being a Mobilizer teacher has its challenges, but I'm now a better teacher because I recognize my specific Mobilizer personality tendencies.

"The biggest thing I noticed was in my relationship with God. I have always wanted to be the one in charge, so it was hard for me to let Him take over my life. But, little by little, I have learned to depend on Him and that has truly been a life-changer in many ways."

Quick Tip for Mobilizers

Though you like to get lessons done quickly, remember your classroom is full of those who work at various speeds.

You might be a SOCIALIZER if…

- You love to live life the fun way, especially when teaching your students.

- You're creative and a storyteller.

- You tend to speak a lot.

- You enjoy attention and approval.

- You're distracted/disturbed when life is no longer fun.

- You like freed up schedules and to be showered with affection.

- Eating out and/or shopping relaxes you.

Socializers love a party and seek the fun element in everything they do. Socializers love people and feel lonely when they are not around them. Taking time to relax and be still is difficult and often requires great discipline for the Socializer personality.

"I am often called the 'fun teacher,'" says Lucy, high school math teacher. "And, it's true, I do like to have a good time, even when I am teaching. Though I like to have fun, it's hard sometimes to focus on the lesson plan and accomplish what I need to in the classroom. Learning I am a Socializer explains a lot. My personality naturally gravitates to the fun and spontaneous way of doing things.

"I've learned that when I want to be more focused, I make a list on my whiteboard each morning of everything I need to accomplish. That way, I can complete more tasks. It's still not always easy and I often have to promise myself lunch with a friend on the coming weekend as a reward for checking everything off my list. Makes me feel good when I can do that!"

Quick Tip for Socializers

The classroom is not a party room. A little structured fun goes a long way as long as you get your work done.

You might be a STABILIZER if...

- You love to live life the easy way.

- You tend to think before you speak.

- You appreciate respect from your students.

- You're supportive, easy going, and work well under pressure.

- You like peace and quiet.

- You're distracted/disturbed when your classroom becomes chaotic.

- Time alone such as watching TV or reading a book relaxes you.

Stabilizers love people yet shy away from conflict and change. Stabilizers are seen as the quiet and relaxed personality. Though the Stabilizer teacher often has the calmest classroom, her lack of excitement in her voice can come across as boring to the Socializer and Mobilizer students. Changing up the tempo and tone helps to keep the students' attention. Stabilizers are kind with most students and they have endless patience in explaining steps in a learning process. The Stabilizer teacher often builds deep relationships with students and, often, becomes a sounding board for his or her students.

"Growing up, my family called me lazy, and I believed them," says Brent. "But once I got into the classroom, I realized I had a lot to offer the students. Learning about my Stabilizer personality validated me as a person and gave me a lot of confidence. I knew I could be a good teacher as long as I voiced my opinions and stuck to my decisions. My style was just as not energetic nor organized as other teachers. My family never understood that I really loved doing activities with them; I just didn't like doing them at the same pace. Knowing I am a Stabilizer has helped me to understand that my slower pace is okay.

With students that is sometimes a big plus. I can take time to encourage those who are struggling with a concept. I can also creatively direct those who have finished their work with an additional research assignment and all are happy. I think knowing the personalities of my students will help me be a better teacher."

Quick Tip for Stabilizers

As a Stabilizer teacher, though you run your class with an easy-going style, remember some students will try to run the class their way. Stand your ground and you'll do great."

You might be an ORGANIZER if...

- You love to live life the right way.

- You're loyal and sensitive to your students.

- You tend to listen more, speak less, and think a lot.

- You're thoughtful and deliberate.

- You're distracted/disturbed when life is imperfect.

- You like quality over quantity.

- Long stretches of silence and plenty of space relaxes you.

Organizers are rule followers who often get labeled as perfectionists! They want assignments done the right way, every day, which makes life a challenge for them personally. Not only do they strive for perfectionism themselves, they also expect it of their students and family. Because of this perfectionism, Organizers may also find it hard to accept others unconditionally. As a deep thinker, the Organizer is often well-grounded in his or her faith. When students need a good listener, the Organizer is probably their person! They are also loyal to a fault and great cheerleaders for their students.

Doug says, "What a self-revelation to discover my personality drives the way I think as a teacher and the way I manage my classroom. Even though our family homeschools, I still want to apply all the great principles of the classroom. I love teaching and knowing my personality and the personalities of my children makes our school time go more smoothly. It's encouraging to know my attention to detail with my students/children is not just a result of my wanting to give them more work. My Organizer personality pays great attention to every point and wants my students to do the same. Understanding that they may not enjoy the research like I do, or feel that every little bit of information is important, really helps my teacher/student relationships.

When I discovered my perfectionist tendencies were a personality trait and not an inborn desire to drive myself and everyone around me crazy, it was liberating. I allowed myself the freedom to be who God created me to be. I was free to accept students for the way they were. It wasn't an overnight thing but as I worked at it, I began to enjoy teaching without the encumbrance of judgment and perfectionism."

Quick Tip for Organizers

Though perfectionism has its place, sometimes it is okay to make an A and not an A+.

"Teachers can change lives with just
the right mix of chalk and challenges."
~Joyce Meyer

Internalize How You Relate To Others

Now that you have identified your dominant personality, let's take a quick look at how your personality affects your teaching style and how you relate to your students.

If you are a Mobilizer teacher:

Be prepared for people to label you as "bossy." As a task-oriented individual who likes control, this label is to be expected. If you see a situation you can improve on by jumping in and directing the actions of your students, you really want to do it. Be aware of this tendency and instead of jumping in uninvited, direct your students to discover ways they can correct the problem themselves and give them enough time to do it.

Checklists are your favorite tool to chart progress toward a goal. Seeing items checked off is an encouragement to you. In the classroom, daily interruptions occur and there are moments that have to be redirected. These interruptions can be frustrating to your Mobilizer personality. Approach it as another challenge for which to find a solution. Involve your students in meeting the challenge. You like knowing things will be done your way and how better for that to happen than for you to do it yourself. However, as a Mobilizer teacher in a class full of varied-personality students, you must try to include them in every learning experience you can. (See the implementing section.)

You're a great teacher and in leadership positions you excel. You will work tirelessly to make sure you do a good job. Your students will appreciate your commitment to learning and desire to see them succeed.

 *If you are a Socializer teacher:*

You will always have a fun classroom. There are bright colors on the wall and uplifting words all over. No matter what the subject, you will find a fun way to teach it. You use your love of people to encourage and help them enjoy life. Be careful though, not to overwhelm your students of other personalities with your upbeat, high-energy. Believe it or not, you can tire them out.

Understand you may also have trouble staying on task when you're working on a specific project. And your students are watching you, especially those who are of the same Socializer personality. They need to see you managing your temptation to scrap the meat of the lesson and focus on the fun. Set up a schedule of mini-rewards along the way to be claimed after class dismisses (phone chat with a friend, browsing through an online catalog, etc.) to keep yourself on track.

Never try to squelch your vibrant, fun-loving personality. Many people wish they could be as extroverted as you are! Your students will be no exception.

 *If you are a Stabilizer teacher:*

You have great ideas but seldom share them because of your introverted tendency. Speak up, because what you have to say is important! Be sure to vary your vocal tone to keep everyone engaged. As a Stabilizer teacher, you must be in front of the class as you lead them to learn, and you may be uncomfortable doing that. Yet, because you understand your calling to teach you can do it. Even though it sometimes takes a lot of your energy to stand there, you will—for the love of your subject and the opportunity to help your students learn.

You were made to be less intense in many ways than other people. Being calm is not a bad thing for a teacher. Capitalize on that personality trait. Don't let someone else's conflict get in the way of your peace. You are the peacemaker, and in being so, you tend to be a solid teacher who is sensitive to the needs of all your students. Stabilizer teachers are easy to get along with and bring a calmness to their classrooms.

If you are an Organizer teacher:

Being task-oriented, you will enjoy the times when your students are working on specific projects—science fairs, term papers, etc. Sometimes the classroom becomes a bit overwhelming because being in a crowd is not your thing. So you may have days when you arrive home ready for some alone time. Allow yourself that time to recharge. Deep down you enjoy your students and want to build relationships with them. It's just not always as easy for you as it is your Socializer and Stabilizer friends.

You're a great listener and once students discover that, they will gravitate to you with their problems and concerns. Your advice is usually well-grounded, researched, and quite often rooted in your faith. You accomplish much because of your attention to detail and deadline.

Ask questions to make sure you understand any part of a conversation you're unsure about. You easily get your feelings hurt because of your sensitivity and many times it's the result of just not clarifying what another teacher or student says.

No Matter Your Personality:

Embrace the full concept of "as far as it depends on you," and understand no matter what personality you are, you have control over your perspective and how you interact with others.

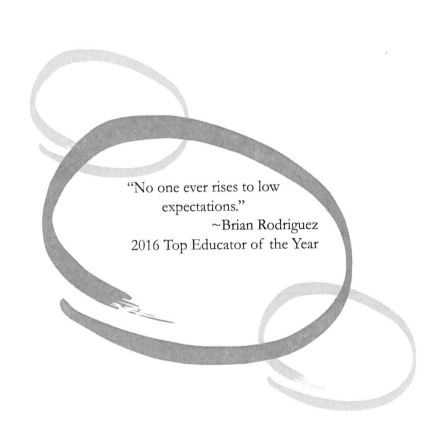

"No one ever rises to low
expectations."
~Brian Rodriguez
2016 Top Educator of the Year

Key Word Identifiers

To help you even more in understanding the personalities quickly, we're including some key word identifiers for each personality.

We've added the words "extrovert" and "fast-responding" for the Mobilizer and Socializer, both of these personalities share these behavior styles but for different reasons. The Mobilizer gains control by his or her extrovert trait while the Socializer gains attention; and the fast-responding Mobilizer, though meticulous, prefers to check off boxes quickly while the free-spirited Socializer is found to be very spontaneous, moving quickly from one thought to another.

The Mobilizer is a Fast-Responding Extrovert

Positive Tendencies

Not Easily Discouraged
Delegates
Independent
Born Leader
Results-oriented
Strong-Willed
Decisive
Confident
Organized
Enthusiastic
Loves a Challenge

Negative Tendencies

Bossy
Impatient
Quick-tempered
Controlling
Inflexible
Domineering
Knows Everything
May be rude, tactless
Demands loyalty
Blunt
Competitive

The Socializer is a Fast-Responding Extrovert

Positive Tendencies

Storyteller
Sense of humor
Enthusiastic
Cheerful
Doesn't Hold Grudges
Touchy Feely
Colorful Dresser
People-oriented
Optimistic
Makes friends quickly
Spontaneous
Creative and colorful

Negative Tendencies

Exaggerates
Undisciplined
Easily Distracted
Egotistical
Loud
Wants Center Stage
Doesn't listen
Overcommits
Overly Talkative
Disorganized
Tends to arrive late
Forgetful
Seeks Social Acceptance

The Stabilizer is a Slow-Responding Introvert

Positive Tendencies

Easy Going
Relaxed and Calm
Competent
Good under pressure
Patient
Good listener
Likes people
Dry sense of humor
Quiet but witty
Humble
Team Player
Supportive
Service-oriented

Negative Tendencies

Indecisive
Would rather watch
Too compromising
Stays uninvolved
Indifferent
Judges
Resists change
Fearful
Worried
Hides Emotions
Stubborn
Low-energy
May sleep a lot

The Organizer is a Slow-Responding Introvert

Positive Tendencies

Thoughtful
Analytical
Serious
Detail-oriented
High Standards
Creative
Appreciative of Beauty
Orderly
Economical
Faithful
Self-disciplined
Neat and Tidy
Compassionate
Loves Charts, Tables, and Graphs
Tends to be right

Negative Tendencies

Moody
Low self-image
Deep need for approval
Standards too high
Hard to please
Too Introspective
Guilt feelings
Insecure socially
Withdrawn
Critical of others
Holds back affection
Perfectionistic
Doesn't Make Friends Easily

Stabilizers and Organizers keep to themselves as introverts. Time spent behind the scenes by himself is pleasing to the Stabilizer; while the Organizer doesn't require the input of others to complete her tasks. The term slow-responding in no fashion relates to the mental prowess of these two personalities. The Organizer takes her time because she dives into the details and research before giving her opinion, while the Stabilizer is fairly laid back and okay with others making decisions. He doesn't get riled up. When he says, "I'm fine," he truly means it.

Remember, this is a quick-guide to the personalities, as such, there may be more questions you want answered. Please don't hesitate to ask us your questions; we love connecting with our readers. You will find our contact information at the back of this book.

"Education is the key to success in life, and teachers make a lasting impact in the lives of their students."
~Solomon Ortiz, former US Representative for Texas' 27th congressional district

Implement What You Have Learned

Without putting your knowledge of the personalities into practice, it is not worth a lot to you or your students. But knowing how to guide and direct students will help them develop into the most successful people they can be. Understanding how to act and react toward them individually can make a big difference.

In an article titled, "Behavior in High School Predicts Income and Occupational Success Later in Life," Marion Spengler, PHD, of the University of Tübingen, says, "Educational researchers, political scientists, and economists are increasingly interested in the traits and skills that parents, teachers, and schools should foster in children to enhance chances of success later in life." Spengler goes on to say, "Our research found that specific behaviors in high school have long-lasting effects for one's later life."[2]

Teaching is an important profession. How many times have you heard the question asked, "Name one person who had a tremendous influence on making you the person you are today?"

Often the answer is a teacher, sometimes from many years ago.

Teachers are shaping lives for years to come, and one of the best tools available to do that is an understanding of the personalities.

Hopefully you are beginning to see how valuable knowledge of the personalities is in the classroom and especially in one-on-one relationships/connections with your students. Now let's take a look at some additional ways you can implement this knowledge in your teaching.

In order to make the most of your knowledge and deepen your relationships, you must know what your strengths and weaknesses are as well as those of your students. Understanding the strengths and weaknesses of other personalities, you will also identify the potential areas of conflict and how to avoid them. You will also know how to approach friends and family in the best way possible to grow your relationships.

For example, Mr. Bart is a strong Socializer teacher who always wants to be around people. He's a fun teacher and his classroom is often called the "party room" by his students. He makes learning fun and has even been known to jump from his desk to illustrate gravity! Most of the time, Mr. Bart loves the encouragement of his Socializer students and doesn't even notice the others in the class who seemed surprised and appalled by his antics.

Georgia is one of his best and high-achieving students. However, Georgia is an Organizer personality and doesn't have much tolerance for the carefree, light-hearted teaching style of her Socializer teacher. She has little use for frivolity and would much prefer spending class time discussing research and finding the deep meaning of the subjects.

Because of his matter-of-fact Mobilizer personality, Chris doesn't enjoy Mr. Bart's attempts to embellish the learning experience. Often he would like to raise his hand and just say, "Get on with it. Tell us what we need to know!"

Chris sits across from Georgia and they often share rolled-eyed glances when Mr. Bart begins one of his Socializer-streaked examples of a concept. They have to admit that it is occasionally entertaining. But neither of them came to school to be entertained.

As Mr. Bart became aware of the different personalities in his classroom, it helped him be more sensitive to the other personalities present. While fun and engaging activities are helpful as illustrations and learning exercises, they don't work for every student. Once Mr. Bart understood that, he was able to integrate various types of activities into his lessons that would benefit everyone.

Mr. Bart and his students strengthened their connections with each other by putting their personality knowledge into action. Read on for more quick-tips to help you link your personality to others.

Linking Personality to Personality

Interacting with the personalities of your students can result in a positive or negative outcome based on how you approach them. Read through the following considerations to better the chances of your classroom connections moving forward in a positive direction.

Mobilizer Teachers Connecting

With Other Mobilizer Students

In this teacher-student connection, the strong personality of the Mobilizer wants control from both sides. Both teacher and student must come to an understanding of the basic teacher/student relationship—that is, the teacher is in charge, and the student must respect and defer to the teacher's authority. A wise teacher will identify with the Mobilizer student's need to be in charge and give him or her a suitable position of leadership. This assignment could be a big responsibility or something as simple as making sure all the classroom library books are properly shelved. If you can encourage your Mobilizer students and their desire to be in charge, you will help them develop leadership skills that will serve them well. This personality type is a good place to put your delegation into action.

Mobilizer students will also appreciate the time you can communicate assignments by using checklists. Because they think this way, a list will help them organize and see a definite end to the assignment. If there is a part of the day's lesson that can involve students, your Mobilizers are great at leading. Give your Mobilizer students a part to read or recite and they will beam. Do you have a student who needs some extra help in one of the subjects? Pair him or her with a Mobilizer student who is strong in that subject. Mobilizer peer tutors are strong-skilled and love helping others. Yet, you may need to encourage them to show compassion when those they tutor don't grasp a concept quickly enough.

Encourage your Mobilizer students to become active listeners and to take notes on your lectures. Asking a question now and then will also help them focus.

With Socializer Students

Your Socializer students and you are different. You tend to have blinders on as you move toward your goal in the fastest and most efficient way possible.

66

If you're working with Socializer students, realize they will lose interest in listening to you and participating in class if some part of the project is not fun and lively.

When teaching, remember your Socializer students need you to create stories that will help them remember what you are teaching. Use fun facts about your subject to create memorable stories. Have contests among your students to help them stay motivated and involved. Suggest ways they can participate. For example, if you are teaching history, teach the facts then challenge the students to act out the story, making sure their details are correct.

Compliment freely. Recognize their enthusiasm and energy as a plus. Even though Socializer students appear self-secure, deep down they crave knowing they're appreciated and loved.

With Stabilizer Students

Using a few warm and fuzzy words will go a long way with Stabilizers. Though they are quiet, they thrive on recognition and verbal encouragement.

Stabilizer students are excellent support people. They can take on many roles, but don't overwhelm them. Offer them class participation roles that are low-key and solid. Think slow and steady. Providing a timeline stating where each part of a project has a due date will be a big help to your Stabilizer students.

Because you are a goal-oriented teacher and find the most direct path to a goal, your Stabilizer students may become overwhelmed and stressed. Remember to give them some breathing room and understand that the paths to their goals must include time for application and reflection.

With Organizer Students

 Remember Organizers tend to be sensitive. They also process at a slower pace than you do. When you ask an Organizer student a question, he or she may have to have a few seconds, or even minutes, to process his or her answer. When working toward a goal, you may tend to overlook Organizer students as possible helpers because they're quiet. But Organizers are great project helpers since they have excellent researching skills and time management. When organizing group projects, it is always good to include at least one Organizer student in each group.

Organizers need to be praised for their part in the project or they won't feel appreciated. Praise is not something you give freely. So make an effort to genuinely praise those working with you.

Socializer Teachers Connecting

With Mobilizer Students

Remember Mobilizers are get-to-the-point, no-nonsense students who want to get their work done as efficiently as possible and just want the facts, no fluff. These students often view your fun-loving approach to education as frivolous and shallow. Mobilizer students appreciate an occasional story but only if it has a strong take away. Otherwise, just teach the subject or comment on the subject at hand. Don't embellish, don't string it out, just tell it like it is. Though, this type of teaching may not be enjoyable for you as a Socializer, you must find a balance with your Mobilizer students so as to create the best learning environment.

Mobilizer students always have the goal in mind. Therefore, older Mobilizer students can help you fill in gaps where you fall a little short. As a Socializer teacher, you may need some help in organization and follow through, so keep in mind this is a strength of your Mobilizer (and Organizer) students. Ask your Mobilizer students to lead study groups. Perhaps you have a student who needs extra help. A Mobilizer student could be just the right mentor. Help your Mobilizer students see there may be more than one way to solve a problem. You're a creative thinker and

69

may come up with solutions the Mobilizer never thought of.

With Other Socializer Students

 Remember you both can't be center stage. Socializers love to be in front of any crowd. However, in a classroom situation, the teacher already has the "stage." Understanding that the Socializer needs some time up front, you can find moments to make that happen either through reading, participating in a play, or having him or her share creative ways to accomplish a homework task, etc.

The Socializer student can sometimes be dubbed the "class clown." This label is not necessarily because the Socializer student is really funny, but because he or she craves attention so badly he or she will use any available antics to be noticed. A student with this personality has tremendous energy and it is up to you, as the Socializer teacher (even though you may think a lot of the conduct of the Socializer student is cute or funny) to channel that energy into something benefiting the classroom.

Find ways to praise your Socializer students. Since you enjoy the attention yourself, you understand the need for it and the deficit that occurs when you go too long without focused attention.

Stabilizers can be your best support in the classroom. The Stabilizer's calm and cool personality can help Socializer teachers remain grounded in the moment. You both enjoy being around people, yet respond differently to those of other personalities.

Remember conflict and "hoopla" are unsettling to your Stabilizer students. They prefer the quieter classroom activities and time spent in individual study. Stabilizers are deep thinkers and may require time to reflect on what is being discussed in the classroom. Be sensitive and don't demand an immediate answer from them. Contemplative time often yields novel approaches to subject areas. However, Stabilizers also benefit from participating in group studies with other personalities since they love their friends.

Some teachers may look upon this personality as lazy. But being thoughtful and laid back should not be confused with being lethargic.

Don't expect your Stabilizer students to excitedly join in activities. They'll want to participate in some of your Socializer teaching examples, but then will need to regroup and refresh with moments of rest and quiet.

Don't rush them to answer. Remember, Organizer students like to think through every response and process every bit of new information before they speak. Give them time to do so. You will most likely receive incredible insight and deep perception, thus adding to your classroom discussion and understanding. You're spontaneous and they're methodical, seeing things in a totally different light, so please don't put them on the spot as it can result in an embarrassing moment for your Organizer.

Organizer students may also be slow to respond to your jokes. Don't force it, just let it be. All humor doesn't seem funny to them. It has to really hit the spot. While for you fun comes easily, remember Organizer students have to work at having a good time.

Organizer students are sensitive so it's a good idea for you to be clear in your expectations to ensure no misunderstandings occur between the two of you. Organizer students tend to take comments at face value. If you make a comment intended to be facetious or taken in a different way, watch the faces of the Organizer students to make sure it was received as meant. Or, be sure to speak more slowly than normal, especially if you're excited. These techniques help both the Organizer and Socializer to grasp your concepts. The Mobilizer will tell you to slow down.

Stabilizer Teachers Connecting

With Mobilizer Students

The goal-oriented Mobilizer student could sometimes create stress unintentionally for you, the Stabilizer teacher, because of this student's focused drive to a goal. This student is so anxious to get to the goal, he or she moves toward it in the most direct way possible. As the Stabilizer teacher, you're always glad to accomplish a goal, but you don't want the student to miss the valuable lessons along the way. Perhaps when working on projects or assignments, you can look for ways to involve the Mobilizer students in a leadership role that still meets your goals. You'll find the efforts you make to establish and build connections with your Mobilizer students a great advantage in helping them learn.

In conversations with Mobilizer students, keep what you say short and to the point. Remember they really don't like all the details you find fascinating.

The best way to prevent a Mobilizer student from trying to run your classroom is to acknowledge his

73

readiness to take charge, "Thank you, John, for always being available to help." Just be sure you have set strong personal boundaries as this is your classroom, not his.

With Socializer Students

As a Stabilizer teacher, you'll find you can relate best to Socializer students when you build good relationships with them. Their outgoing differences can sometimes seem extreme, but if the classroom connection is established with respect, you'll be able to communicate and even encourage each other. Stabilizer teachers often enjoy the energy and flashiness of the Socializer as long as it is appropriate for the classroom. However, after a day filled with Socializer students, you'll often need to go home and rest!

As you maximize your connections with your Socializers, you'll recognize how creative those students are. Ask your Socializer student for ideas as to how to make a lesson fun and more memorable. You may be surprised at how many good suggestions you receive.

Another consideration in understanding your personality better—every once in a while give in to the invitations of your Socializer friends to go out in a group. Your love of people will surface and will be appreciated.

With Other Stabilizer Students

Though both are slow processors, the Stabilizer to Stabilizer can become a fast connection combination. You truly get each other's style and need for a peaceful work environment. Stabilizer teachers enjoy relating to the Stabilizer students and using their time together during the school day almost as an oasis. The Stabilizer teacher can enjoy a moment with a Stabilizer student who really understands him or her.

As a teacher to Stabilizer students, it will benefit the entire class to recognize the calm, often quiet Stabilizer students are great resources and bring great wisdom to the classroom in their own way and timing.

With Organizer Students

You'll find the organizer personality appreciates your love for all students and desire to see them succeed. As you, the Stabilizer teacher, present many different perspectives on subjects, the Organizer student will likely interject questions as a result of processing each of those. Appreciate the Organizer students' desire to fully understand and fully process, a trait not all your students will possess. When creating group exercises in the classroom, ensure an Organizer student is included in every group. He or she will help the group stick to deadlines as well as making sure their facts are accurate, offering a lot of data to back it up.

Stabilizer teachers need to keep in mind your Organizer students tend to be perfectionists. Don't belittle that. Encourage those students to work hard to get their work as perfect as possible then move on. Organizer students have been known to take far too much time to complete their projects because of this attribute.

Organizer Teachers Connecting

With Mobilizer Students

Mobilizer students share attention to detail with their Organizer teachers. The Mobilizer student's drive to the finish line may outshine your Organizer love of research and depth. Mobilizer students are hard workers and want to get assignments done quickly and correctly. Once these students learn what pleases the teacher, they will work with that in mind.

Organizer teachers can be overly sensitive. Don't let the abrupt manner of the Mobilizer student make you feel inadequate, unimportant, or wrong in the way you teach. Understand that the Mobilizer personality is fast-paced and bullet-point focused. It really isn't personal.

With Socializer Students

You may feel inclined to roll your eyes at the energy and frivolity of the Socializer. When this student makes jokes, the Organizer teacher can easily get his or her feelings hurt if they are the brunt of the joke. Other times the Organizer teacher wishes he or she, too, could be as carefree and see life through some not-so-serious lenses. It's difficult for the Organizer teacher to let go and have fun with his or her Socializer students.

The Organizer teacher would be wise to have his or her Socializer students in on the planning stages of a project. The Socializer energy and creative processing carries over to every part of his or her school experience and helps others to get excited when they may not do so ordinarily.

But remember, Organizers thrive on time alone. If you find yourself being short with your students, take a look at how much time and energy you have been expending on a project or explaining a subject. Perhaps, you need to retreat to the teacher's lounge during your next break or planning period to recharge your batteries.

With Stabilizer Students

Organizer teachers would do well to build a good relationship with Stabilizer students. Once the Organizer teacher has an understanding of his Stabilizer student's easy-going approach to education, things will go more smoothly. Never overwhelm Stabilizer students with too many decisions or assignments at one time. Give them space and lots of time to contemplate their path of accomplishing the assignments.

Allow your Stabilizer students the freedom to be who they are and work in the manner they choose. Younger students won't have the freedom to change location or work in an unsupervised area of the classroom. But older Stabilizer students will appreciate the opportunity to go to the library or work independently of the crowd. Providing frequent breaks for your Stabilizer students will pay off in more focused group time.

With Other Organizer Students

Organizer teachers and Organizer students work well together because they agree on many things. They love attention to detail and deep research. To avoid misunderstanding, make sure all Organizers fully know what is expected with each assignment as in the length of the project, minimum number of references required, and the deadline. As one yourself, you know that the Organizer loves details.

The perfectionist aspect of the Organizer's personality could create conflict between an Organizer teacher and an Organizer student. When working with your Organizer students, stress the need to reach the goal you have set in the allotted time. Encourage him or her to keep working toward the goal rather than making sure every little detail is perfect.

"Teachers, I believe, are the most responsible and important members of society because their professional efforts affect the fate of the earth."
~Helen Caldicott

Using Your Knowledge of the LINKED Personalities in the Classroom

Short answer to when to use your knowledge of the LINKED® Personalities in the classroom—all day long! Have you ever been surprised by an action or reaction of one of your students? Perhaps you didn't stop to think the behavior was a result of that student's personality characteristics mixed with your personality interaction.

In this section, we are looking at where and when you can use personality knowledge in your classroom to benefit the students, make your teaching more effective, and to improve relational connections with your students.

For instance, Mrs. Smithfield started the day with an announcement that it was time to prepare for the annual science fair. Her students knew the fair was part of the spring curriculum, so it was not a surprise to them that it was time to start working on it.

Students in Mrs. Smithfield's class had varied reactions truly characteristic of their personalities.

Greg listened carefully as Mrs. Smithfield gave all the details of the fair. Then she moved to specifics for each individual entry. Before Mrs. Smithfield was even finished, Greg had begun a checklist of possible projects he could do and the items he would need for each. He was confident he could do a good job and eager to get started.

Harriet, on the other hand, also listened but her mind wandered, landing on one key word—fair. "Fair" sounded like a great event—lots of fun for everyone. She is already thinking of how to get several of her friends to attend together. Why, they might even make a day of it and go out to eat! Maybe one of her friends could even help her with her project. Or better yet, they could do a joint project.

Joe listened carefully as Mrs. Smithfield talked about the science fair. His mind occasionally drifted onto a "rabbit trail" when she mentioned something sparking another thought. Joe tried his best to listen so he would know the details of the science fair, but it wasn't easy to stay focused. He would think for a while and decide later what his project would be.

Miriam got excited when Mrs. Smithfield brought up the subject of the science fair. Miriam already knew what her topic would be and listened closely to make sure it fit in Mrs. Smithfield's parameters. Miriam would start collecting her needed supplies and make a list of possible research interviews she needed as soon as she got home.

Can you see the different approaches these students had to the science fair? Can you guess what personality each of these students are? If you decided Greg was a Mobilizer, you were correct. Harriet, our Socializer, was already planning to make the science fair the fun event of the spring. Always the Stabilizer, Joe was thinking in his own quiet way and would get around to formulating a plan when he felt like it. Miriam thrived on planning her project and executing it to perfection. If you pegged her as the Organizer, you were right about her.

How to Encourage Your Students

Whether you are a Mobilizer, Socializer, Stabilizer, or Organizer teacher, you can use the following tips and strategies to encourage and equip your students according to their natural personality bent. Remember to tap into your strengths as we move forward in order to implement what works for you to maximize your classroom connections.

Mobilizer Students

Some of your strongest and/ or headstrong students will be Mobilizers. Because of their desire to reach their goals, Mobilizer students sometimes overlook the relational areas of the classroom; in the process they tend to run over others in the classroom. Understanding the Mobilizer's **confident, decisive, and unemotional** approach to the school work will give you insight as to how to best approach these students and help them grow. Though not easily discouraged because of their "I can do this by myself" attitude, Mobilizer students need to be encouraged to include others. They always welcome a pat on the back from the teacher.

Remember Your Mobilizer Students

- Need encouragement to develop good listening skills. Their minds often go directly to the end result, and they occasionally miss some of the important points along the way.
- Are excellent mentors for other students needing help.
- Enjoy being put in charge of study groups, research groups, or any student group.
- Believe they could teach the class themselves. Every now and then, you may have to gently remind them it's your classroom.

List the names of your Mobilizer students below.

_____

_____

_____

_____

Socializer Students

With a flare for fashion, fun, and the dramatic, there will be no mistake recognizing your Socializer students. It's good to remember despite positioning themselves in front of the class at any opportunity, Socializers need individual attention from you as well. Teachers will do well to make the most of the creativity of their Socializer students. If you can keep them involved with a carrot-of-fun, they will be able to focus better on the subject or project at hand.

Remember Your Socializer Students

- Need individual words of encouragement. The class reaction is an encouragement in many ways, but to have the teacher praise you individually is a tremendous bonus to the Socializer student.
- Benefit from your creative stories to help them learn.
- Love to be involved in study groups. In doing so, they can see and mimic how other students learn while enjoying a fun time of belonging to the group.
- Are quick to volunteer when the teacher needs a helper but need encouragement and fun reminders to follow through.

List the names of your Socializer students below.

_____

_____

_____

_____

Stabilizer Students

The Stabilizer students can be some of your most conscientious students. But at times they may need a little push to initiate a project and to complete their goals. Stabilizers enjoy class time because they can fit in without much participation. They rarely speak up and only after plenty of time for reflection and thought will they offer an opinion.

Remember Your Stabilizer Students

- Like to contribute to the class discussion but often must be prompted or called upon.
- Welcome help setting deadlines for projects.
- Will find more success if you help them create bite-sized goals to strive toward.
- Shy away from any kind of conflict. Even a heated discussion in debate class can cause your Stabilizer students to shut down.

List the names of your Stabilizer students below.

_____

_____

_____

_____

Organizer Students

You will find that Organizer students are generally cooperative students. Their love of organization and research translates into good learning experiences. Organizer students could be the hardest to get to know personally because of their social reservation. But you will find them loyal classroom supporters once you have them on your side.

Remember, your Organizer students:

- Are team players therefore they make good group study members and mentors.
- Don't like surprises. They prefer you stick to your established schedule.
- Sometimes have trouble making decisions.
- Like to think before they answer questions.

List the names of your Organizer students below.

_____

_____

_____

_____

How to Encourage and Equip Your Students' Parents

As a teacher, you not only deal with students all day, but on occasion you need to interact with their parents concerning disciplinary actions. Here are some quick tips to consider when you need to reply, explain, and support the different parenting personalities.

The Mobilizer Parent

Reply with confidence in your position. Focus directly on the student's actions, not his or her character.

Explain with brief bullet points, supplying a plan of action to help the student succeed.

Support by including a timeline with the objectives and goal clearly stated.

The Socializer Parent

Reply with a positive and friendly outlook. Give the parent time to talk and ask questions.

Explain by providing a plan of action to help his or her child succeed. Allow time for a sharing of feelings on the parent's part.

Support by suggesting incentives for solving the discipline issue. Always use a positive approach.

The Stabilizer Parent

Reply in a gentle fashion. Keep a nonthreatening posture and if possible, remain seated and patient to the best of your ability.

Explain with assurance everything will work out. Give a clear easy plan and time for this parent time to process.

Support by coming alongside as a team player. Reassure him he's not alone and be patient, which allows breathing time for the parent.

The Organizer Parent

Reply calmly, knowing this parent tends to be negative up front and cautious.

Explain with logic. Stay the course by providing as much documentation as possible.

Support this parent by assuring your support and offering a step-by-step plan of success for his or her child.

"The art of teaching is the art of assisting discovery."

~Mark Van Doren

Pulitzer Prize-winning American poet

Consider the following scenarios and how you might respond based on your personality.

Andrew's Story

Mrs. Gee's kindergarten class was lining up at the door to go to the gym. They had just completed their seated circle time and were ready for an activity requiring movement.

"Line up at the door please," she said.

Andrew turned around from his position at the door. "Everyone line up."

Mrs. Gee placed her hand on Andrew's shoulder. "Thank you, Andrew."

Shari and Brinn lingered in the home center on their way to the line. It was their favorite station and they especially loved to play beauty parlor in the kitchen.

"Girls, come on and line up," Andrew shouted for good measure.

Once again, Mrs. Gee lightly touched Andrew's shoulder. He smiled up at Mrs. Gee.

"Boys and girls, let's remember when we walk down the hall to be quiet and not disturb the other classrooms."

"Yeah, and keep the line straight," Andrew added.

Mrs. Gee looked down at Andrew. "Andrew, I really appreciate you wanting to help. But I am the teacher, and I need the boys and girls to listen to me. From now on, please let me take care of giving instructions."

Andrew nodded. "Sorry, Mrs. Gee."

What do you think Andrew's personality is? How would you handle him if he were in your classroom?

_____

_____

_____

_____

Even as a kindergartner, Andrew's strong Mobilizer personality wanted to be in charge of his class. Mrs. Gee was a sensitive teacher and didn't want to squelch Andrew's leadership ability. But she also wanted to make sure his desire to be in control didn't overshadow his respect for her authority.

95

Mr. Davie's Story

Mr. Davie stood in front of his class. "I'd like everyone to turn in outlines for your research papers tomorrow. Then Friday, please give me a fleshed-out plan for writing your papers. It will be due in four weeks. If this project seems overwhelming to you, please see me after class, and I will help you create a plan for your paper."

Looking around the class, he saw different reactions.

Ruth raised her hand. "How long does this paper have to be? Couldn't we just talk about what we learned and sort of give a speech about it? I'm sure everyone would love to hear the stories about my subject."

Sam sat silently in his seat. Mr. Davie had this class long enough to know the thought of writing an entire paper in four weeks was a bit overwhelming to Sam and a few others.

Still others already had their pencils dancing on their paper, eager anticipation on their faces.

Mr. Davie looked around at the class. "Don't let this paper become a burden. You all need to learn how to do a research paper, and I am here to help. If you have any questions, please let me know."

Why do students of different personalities approach research papers so differently? What is Mr. Davie's personality and how can you see him helping his students make this research paper assignment a positive experience?

_____
_____
_____
_____

Twins Tara and Charlotte

Tara and Charlotte were twins. Everyone expected them to be just alike. But that wasn't exactly true of these sisters, especially in the classroom.

Super Socializer Tara couldn't wait to get to class every day. After all, her best friends were there. The moment she stepped on campus, she was surrounded by chattering peers. Tara was content to catch up with that group of friends until she spied others walking across the parking lot. Tara didn't want to miss talking with any class member that day.

Charlotte, on the other hand, saw school differently. This Organizer wanted to learn and all the socialization just got in the way of that. She longed to be a doctor when she grew up, so making sure she did her best in school was an important part of meeting her goal. Even though this was her senior year and many senior students considered this the year to have fun, Charlotte never relaxed the high standards she had set for herself. When she passed her sister in the halls during class change, Tara was usually too busy to speak. Occasionally she got a wave, a nod, and a quick, "Hey, Char," and then Tara turned back to her friends. Charlotte continued her purposeful walk to the next class, usually alone.

Students approach school and the avenue to their goals differently, even twins.

If you had students like Tara and Charlotte in your classes, how would you approach them to assure they receive the best education possible?

_____

_____

_____

_____

"Your role as a leader is even more important than you might imagine. You have the power to help people become winners."
~Ken Blanchard

Lasting Links to Everyday Life

As we wrap up, consider these final words of personality-specific encouragement:

Mobilizer
Delegate with love and appreciation.
Temper your directness with a smile.
Lead others with boldness and courage.

Socializer

Enjoy your fun-loving ways.
Lavish your love on people.
Use good judgment when being spontaneous.

Stabilizer

Be confident in volunteering your services.

Find another steadfast friend to relax with.

Use your patience to manage conflict among others.

Organizer

Temper your perfectionist bent with humility.

Allow others freedom to be themselves.

Reach out to others and cultivate friendships.

Remember, this book is a quick-guide to the personalities: as such, there may be more questions you want answered. Please don't hesitate to ask us your questions; we love connecting with our readers. You will find our contact information at the back of this book.

Check out the following Q&A and let us know other questions you have.

Q & A with the Authors

Q—Why do you think a study of the personalities is so important to educators?
A—Knowing more about your personality, frees you to walk in your strengths not your weaknesses. It's human nature to compare ourselves to others, just like those children who often look up to their heroes, saying, "I want to be Superman when I grow up."

Not everyone was made to be Superman or the professor you may desire to emulate. Once you realize you were made to be you, you are free to be the best you you can be.

Understanding the personalities of others socially or in your classroom allows you to interact and teach them in a way that allows them to be who they were meant to be enabling you to accept them as such. You no longer pass judgment on others because they aren't just like you. You realize they have strengths and weaknesses and by incorporating personality-based teaching, you help them be their best as well.

Q—At what age does a person's personality become obvious to others?
A—Personality can be determined at a young age. Once you are aware of the characteristics of the different personalities, you realize some traits begin

to exhibit themselves in infancy and toddlerhood. Therefore, teachers of all ages can benefit from this study of the personalities.

Observing children at play, I'm sure you've noticed some play together well and some don't. The way in which they play is telling. Sarah dumps her blocks out in a pile by turning the bucket over. Kyle takes each block out of the bucket one by one and strategically places them on the floor. Rebecca arranges hers in a creative pattern while, Justin, doesn't seem to care how they are arranged. Based on their God-given nature, children are Socializers, Mobilizers, Organizers, and Stabilizers.

Q—How can all this information make a difference in my classroom? We all have to get the job done.
A—Knowing the personalities of yourself and your students allows you to work with them and help them learn in the best possible way. Understanding their learning styles allows you to match them to the best possible assignments. When you are able to do that, your classroom will run more smoothly and efficiently and you will have happier and more productive students and parents.

For example, Mrs. Grantham was a Socializer teacher, spending all day long in a classroom with limited flexibility and little time for socializing. Once she learned how to integrate her Socializer personality into her teaching style, instead of feeling like she was fighting a losing battle of non-interactive dreariness all day, Mrs. Grantham became a different person. Understanding she had students who didn't appreciate always approaching learning from the fun viewpoint encouraged Mrs. Grantham to incorporate other learning styles into her lessons, satisfying all of her students' personalities.

Q—How does understanding the personalities impact my daily life?

A—Every day, we talk with people, whether in person or through technology. Think about the miscommunication that occurs when we speak. Most of it can be eliminated if we speak to the personality instead of the person.

Speaking to the personality of the person helps me, a Mobilizer, curb my reactions so I can consider a better path instead of my gut impression. I take a breath (albeit a second or two) and allow a response to come out, based on who they are and who I am, instead of words that could possibly ignite hurt feelings.

Q—So you're suggesting I consider the other person first?

A—Yes. We are to love others as we love ourselves, therefore considering the way another individual receives you is important in linking together with who they are. You will find the seconds it takes to think of others first will save you and them a lot of conflict. You may learn a bit more about their backstory as well.

Q—I have high numbers in two of the personality types, is that normal?
A—Absolutely! There is natural blending of the personalities; Mobilizer-Socializer, Socializer-Stabilizer, Stabilizer-Organizer, and Organizer-Mobilizer. In some cases, other combinations occur as in Mobilizer/Stabilizer and Socializer/Organizer. These combinations usually happen based on learned behavior. For more information on this topic, check out our free Blended Personalities download at LinkedPersonalities.com.

Be sure to visit www.LinkedPersonalities.com and www.facebook.com/linkedpersonalites for podcasts, teachings, and coaching opportunities.

Assessment Key

	Mobilizer	Socializer	Stabilizer	Organizer
1	a	b	d	c
2	a	b	d	c
3	c	a	d	b
4	d	c	a	b
5	b	a	d	c
6	c	a	d	b
7	c	a	d	b
8	d	b	a	c
9	c	b	d	a
10	c	d	b	a
11	d	a	b	c
12	a	b	d	c
13	a	d	c	b
14	d	a	c	b
15	d	a	c	b
16	b	c	a	d
17	b	d	c	a
18	a	d	b	c
19	c	b	d	a
20	a	b	d	c
21	a	b	d	c
22	c	a	d	b
23	d	c	b	a
24	b	d	c	a
25	a	d	c	b
26	a	d	b	c
Total				
	Mobilizer	Socializer	Stabilizer	Organizer

Get-to-know-you
Quick Student Questionnaire

Take a few moments and circle your best fit for each question.

Would you describe yourself as
- a - The get-it-done person
- b - The life-of-the-party person
- c - The keep-it-peaceful person
- d - The keep-everything-in-order-person

When you get home from school, you finish your homework
- a - Right away
- b - Before going to bed, making sure everything is correct
- c - The next morning before school
- d - When you're reminded to

What type of homework assignments do you prefer
- a - Assignments I can finish quickly
- b - Research assignments
- c - Group assignments
- d - Easy assignments

I tend to make new friends
- a - Easily
- b - Cautiously

c - Reservedly

d - Rarely

Friends would call you

a - Low-key

b - Courageous

c - Neat and Tidy

d - Spontaneous

Life is good when

a - You're in control

b - You have order

c - You're having fun

d - You're at peace

When you are in a group

a - You talk a lot

b - You tell people what to do

c - You think carefully before you talk

d - You prefer listening to others

Meet the Two Lindas

Linda Gilden

My introduction to the personalities came over twenty years ago and was life-changing. On discovering I was a purposeful, melancholy Organizer, I learned perfectionism is one of my traits. I also learned that not only did I expect perfectionism of myself but of everyone around me. That was a real eye-opener. It helped me learn not to be so hard on myself or others. Once I understood my perfectionism, I was free to be me and let others do the same. My relationships with friends and family improved dramatically as I allowed those around me to be who God intended them to be. Welcome to the exciting world of personalities. You are about to go on an amazing journey!

~Linda Gilden (Rose) - Author, Speaker, Writing Coach, Writer Conference Director, Certified Advanced Personalities Trainer and Consultant, Teacher, and Instructor of kindergarteners through college students.

Linda Goldfarb

My fifteen-year journey of studying and teaching the personalities has grown me as a powerful Mobilizer. I've learned to temper my pointing, soften my tone, and dress to be more inviting as a speaker. As a writer, I capture my audience's attention by using easy-to-understand words, adding stories, showing my research and always making a point. As a board certified Christian life coach, I guide my clients, specific to their personalities, resulting in higher goals reached in a shorter timeframe. My personal relationships have grown to a deeper level as well. Now, it's your turn. I hope you're ready to connect with others in ways you've never done before!

~Linda Goldfarb (Goldie) - Author, International Speaker, Founder and Instructor of Parenting Awesome Kids, Board Certified Advanced Life Coach, Certified Advanced Personalities Trainer, and Consultant.

Acknowledgments

We are so blessed to be able to share with you the *LINKED® for Educators Quick Guide to Personalities*, book two in our *LINKED* series.

Our families are our head cheerleaders. We love you and appreciate you. The sacrifices you have made for the writing of this book have not gone unnoticed.

To Bold Vision Books. What a blessing to work with such a professional team to whom only excellence will do. Thank you for believing this project can change lives.

To **Brenda Blanchard and Dalene Parker.** Your excellent eyes for detail on this guide and editorial expertise are a blessing. Thank you.

To our writers groups, educators, and others who have brainstormed with us and shared ideas. Thank you.

Jonathan Bishop. Thank you for using your creativity to birth our emoji personality people.

Thank you, Florence Littauer, Gerry Wakeland, and the CLASS family. Because of you, we have an understanding of the personalities that has allowed us to build and grow relationships in a deeper way.

Acknowledgements are never complete without recognizing the direction of the Creator of all. Thank You, God, for the opportunity to be Your messengers.

References

1 https://www.sciencedaily.com/
releases/2014/12/141217090812.htm - Dr Arthur Poropat
from Griffith's School of Applied Psychology

2 http://www.apa.org/news/press/releases/2018/02/high-
school-behavior.aspx - by Marion Spengler, PhD, University
of Tübingen, Rodica Ioana Damian, PhD, University of
Houston, and Brent W. Roberts, PhD, University of Illinois
at Urbana-Champaign University of Tübingen. Journal of
Personality and Social Psychology, published Feb. 26, 2018.
http://www.apa.org/pubs/journals/releases/psp-
pspp0000185.pdf

More LINKED® PERSONALITY RESOURCES FOR YOU

Visit LINKEDPersonalities.com for more
information and to order
LINKED Personality Assessments.

Watch for more Quick Guides Coming Soon.

LINKED Quick Guide to Personalities for Parents
Maximizing Family Connections One Link at a Time

LINKED Quick Guide to Personalities for Writers
Maximizing Connections with Your Audience and
Industry Professionals One Link at a Time

LINKED Quick Guide to Personalities for Leaders
Maximizing Relational Skills One Link at a Time

LINKED Quick Guide to Personalities for Teens
Maximizing Relationships One Link at a Time